CAT CUTS

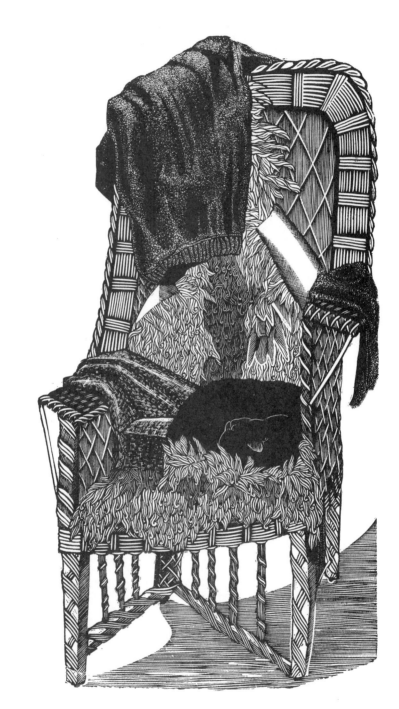

Sarah van Niekerk

CAT CUTS

A collection of engravers' cats
compiled by Miriam Macgregor

SILENT BOOKS

CAMBRIDGE

ACKNOWLEDGEMENT

Thanks are due to the following people for their kind permission to reproduce the engravings listed below.

A.D. Quickenden for page 39; Lesley Weissenborn for page 41; Simon Brett for page 50; Brian North Lee for both prints on page 51; Janet Stone for page 56 (below); and to Theresa Whistler for the extract from *Rushavenn Time* on page 49.

First published in Great Britain 1989
by Silent Books, Swavesey, Cambridge CB4 5RA

Reprinted twice

Each engraving © copyright the engraver in the first instance and reproduced with permission of the artist or his heirs; and of other parties as acknowledged above. In those cases where it has not been possible to make contact, apologies are offered and parties concerned are invited to write to the publisher. The selection and introduction © copyright Miriam Macgregor 1989.

ISBN 1 85183 017 0

Typeset by Goodfellow & Egan, Cambridge
Printed in Great Britain by St Edmundsbury Press,
Bury St Edmunds, Suffolk

All engravings are reproduced actual size with the exception of:
The endpapers, William Rawlinson, original size 152 × 203mm
Pamela Hughes, page 18, original size 102 × 133mm
Enid Marx, page 46, original size 140 × 146mm
Rosemary Myers, page 25, 121 × 152mm
Jennifer Mathison, page 42, original size 127 × 146mm
Clifford Webb, page 50, original size 279 × 229mm

FOREWORD

Whenever I visit a wood-engraver there is nearly always a cat lurking in the background (or basking in the foreground, as often as not) and this collection of prints forms a small celebration of this evident affinity.

Because wood-engraving can be a chilly occupation, a cat curled up on the lap is a marvellous source of warmth and because, of course, he must never be disturbed, one is anchored there and obliged to face up to difficult passages rather than procrastinate with endless cups of tea. As a gentle rumble mingles with the soft crunch of the graver, woodchips slowly gather on the fur . . . and then, quite suddenly, he's off – the ungrateful creature – always confident, however, of a welcomed return.

Reading through the engravers' comments, it seems that one thing the majority of these cats have in common is that they reach a ripe old age – which only proves that, if you are a cat and you belong to a wood-engraver, life is nothing but a lap of roses.

Miriam Macgregor

John O'Connor

For Archie

John O'Connor

Various nieces when visiting us at a time when we had no less than seven cats including a seal-point Siamese, were dressing up in Indian silks and inexpensive beads. It was a short step to decorating patient cats with ropes of glass beads and brilliant pendants. For some time the cats thus treated seemed totally unaware of their courtly appearance and it was that acceptance of the jewels with an air of superior resignation that first demanded a record of the occasion.

Gwenda Morgan

Simon Brett

Mr Webster is a museum curator in New Zealand and the bookplate was commissioned as a 'thankyou' for his help in genealogical researches. The loom is a play on his name. All I knew was that the cat, with its splodgy face, was the most important thing in his life, so had to be included. It's the only cat I've done.

Cordelia Jones

Cordelia Jones

I first saw Camouflage – or rather, at first I did not see her – lying in a rose bed in a front garden in Blossomgate on my way back from school. She was washing herself. Camouflage is not an ordinary tabby; she is brindled all over her body the colour of a wild rabbit, rather darker along the spine and with some dark spots arranged very beautifully on her creamy stomach. There are stripes on her legs and also on her tail, and her face is very pointed with the most enormous ears. Each ear is very pointed too, and at the tip it is finished with a little quiff of hair which gives her a rather wild look, not like the ordinary stolid domesticated cat. Her colouring makes it almost impossible to see her at times, which is why I called her Camouflage; I did think of calling her 'The Speaker' because she is such a conversational cat, but she seemed to recognise 'Camouflage' much better, almost as if it really was her name, so Camouflage she became.

The first time I saw her I almost didn't see her, and it was only because she moved that I saw her at all. And then, naturally, I stopped and watched her. She soon noticed I was watching her and, tossing back her head, greeted me with a rather affronted miaow, as if to say, 'Have you never seen a cat washing herself before? Have you no better manners than to stand and stare like that?' However, after very thoroughly washing her face, she decided to make my acquaintance. She strolled over and jumped on the garden wall, and, talking all the time, rubbed herself against me and got herself stroked.

Thus began the story of *A Cat called Camouflage* and now I can't really remember which were the fictional doings I made up for my half-Abyssinian cat and which were the real things that she did which inspired me to write around her a novel for older children. Two things are certain, however: one, that she was a cat of character; and two, that she was very beautiful, forever slipping into new elegant – or inelegant – poses that made me reach for my sketch-book. But of course she was far too curious to let me draw her without immediately coming to inspect what I was doing. I have boxes and boxes of half-finished scribbles, page after page, while she washed the most inaccessible parts of her triple-jointed body or suckled the many litters of kittens she produced in a long and happy career. Now that she is gone – she was a child of the '60s – I am still working through the sketches and finding inspiration for more wood engravings, but the three you see here are some of the original ones I did twenty years ago to illustrate the book.

Edwina Ellis

Our cats in 1981; the front one was a cream Burmese nuisance who dismantled the house in his short life and is still remembered by the neighbours who caught him dragging their Sunday joint out of their front door. Other neighbours gave us the seven-year-old and homeless Siamese 'to quieten him down' – to no avail, but we still have her, reckoned to be around eighteen now and *very* quiet.

Pamela Hughes

Living Room. I engraved this room because I have always loved it, and I do enjoy interiors. There were really only two cats – a Siamese called *Lennox*, and *Daisy* a Burmese kitten – but having done a number of drawings of them, I decided to put four in the picture.

Pamela Hughes

19

Yvonne Skargon

Oscar, September 1973–April 1989. When you are fifteen years old *and* have collaborated in a book with Oscar Wilde, a little complacency and an inclination to turn one's back on the world may be forgiven?

Hilary Paynter

Summer Field, 1975. Started and finished in an afternoon, 'Summer Field' was engraved for pleasure, and drawn from memories. *Topsy* the cat was named after a beloved rag doll made by my mother from a pair of my father's uniform socks. Lean, black and slinky, affectionate, adored and missed.

Sister Margaret Tournour

'Kitten' is not any particular kitten, but I engraved it hoping to capture a little of the playful innocence and mischievous wonder that kittens are.

Sue Scullard

My cat was called *Featherstone-Hough*, and he died at the age of seventeen. He was really black and white and patchy, but for the purpose of this engraving I thought it best to leave him black, as a witch's cat should be. Perhaps he would have preferred to be black himself, as his conspicuous markings along with his portly figure, made it difficult for him to catch birds.

Mary Speaight

Miranda – a small female tabby, chosen from a box of kittens in Petticoat Lane. She lived for nineteen years and had a strong territorial claim to the lap of my husband, who once dedicated one of his books to her: 'In Memory of Miranda, who tried to stop me writing it'.

Rosemary Myers

Margaret Theakston

Cat day. Heathcliff is renowned for his falls. His most spectacular was from a second-storey window on to the pavement below. Needless to say, at the first opportunity he went straight back to sleep on the same window ledge.

Margaret Theakston

Cat Night. Corri is gentle and loving in the house but the garden is her own territory and she will commit murder to keep out intruders.

John Lawrence

All my images of cats are based on one cat, *Miscka*, who died at the end of last year, aged eighteen. So far we don't seem able to replace her.

BRIAN ✳ NORTH ✳ LEE
JUVENILIA

·DAISY·DAISY·COME·
BE·MY·VALENTINE·

John Lawrence

Peter Forster

Tom, the poetical cat.

Is wood-engraving an Art or a Craft – or a Therapy – or is it, like having sex, or knitting, or reading a newspaper, simply a method of amusing cats? It is difficult to engrave if a cat is sitting on the block or has its nose two inches from the sharp end. Bewick in his memoir describes in detail the trouble he had with Ferruginous Ducks trying to hatch his sandbag, and George Tute today is said to be greatly inconvenienced by sheep. Cats take the most active interest in the actual process of wood-engraving, the manipulation of the block on the bag, the exact angle of the Anglepoise, the orderly disposition of tools. They take as much interest in the finished result as do most publishers, most galleries and most people. Cats are absolutely unique in that they never call a wood-engraving a 'woodcut', though it would be as pointless explaining the difference between plank and end grain to them as to anyone else.

Peter Forster

Beth Krommes

Reading in the Tub. The cat pictured is *Willie*, who is orange with a white belly. As a kitten he loved to splash in the tub but now acts quite aloof when I call him to come play in the water. He's at his most affectionate and needs to be sitting on my lap when I'm working on a drawing or writing a letter.

Beth Krommes

Snowshoeing. I made this engraving of my husband Dave, our cat *Willie* and myself as a New Year's card for friends and family. Willie can't manoeuvre very well in the deep snow and often needs to be carried when we are snowshoeing.

Rosalind Bliss

Tabby Mylius, who liked posing for me, lived in Camberwell. Whilst travelling to Scotland for his holidays, the family stopped in Leeds and Tabby Mylius went for a walk and never came back. We can only hope that he found a nice new home.

Lines for a Siamese Cat, *Suki*

Sat chit ananda
The cat sat on the mat,
She begat
A purry furry
Friendship,
Blue-eyed
Brown-pointed
Human-like she cried.

You who reigned
Over the Egyptian priests
Ruled in my home
Queen of the hearth
And terror of the field-side,
Guardian of my child.

Shirley Mungapen

35

Richard Shirley Smith

This bookplate was engraved for Benoit Junod, while he was serving as cultural attaché at the Swiss Embassy, hence William Tell's apple. It incorporates his cats *Tango* and *Gribouille*.

Richard Shirley Smith

Portrait of Pépé, 1980. He came to live in Blewbury following his parents' departure for Gibraltar. He was marmalade with white gloves and bib, always at the ready. A close companion during engraving, I later found he mistook my desk lamp for a lady's hair-drier and liked to warm his ears.

Richard Shirley Smith

The artists' cats, 1981. Mr Pipkin, the white fluffy kitten, took Pépé to be his mother from the moment he emerged from the shoebox, in spite of many friendly high-speed chases round the house. He eclipsed my Blewbury Festival Open House Exhibition as everyone only wanted to buy him.

Agnes Miller Parker

Nicholas Johnson

Fighting Cats. The white one is *Timothy White II*, who is afraid of his food. The other was *Speedy* (who should have been – she died from eating a poisoned rat). Once, when walking down the lane looking for her we called 'Speedy... Speedy... Speedy' only to be confronted by a tired and limping jogger, who was not amused.

Hellmuth Weissenborn

Jennifer Mathison

Pud, elegant and fastidious tabby, determined to cause maximum inconvenience to the family with whom she condescends to live.

'Vigilante' Thomas – black as basalt – always looking over his shoulder for imaginary dangers.

Jennifer Mathison

Ulla Frisch

The Lino-Cat came out of the blue as I was listening to the Mendelssohn Violin Concerto. He has a melting tone as he plays his cat's whiskers. (No cat-gut for him or the Quartette.)

Ulla Frisch

The kittens in the toy basket are *Tiger* (the outraged black) and
Thistledown, who belonged to my daughter. They were fighting for
room in her heart as well as space in the basket.

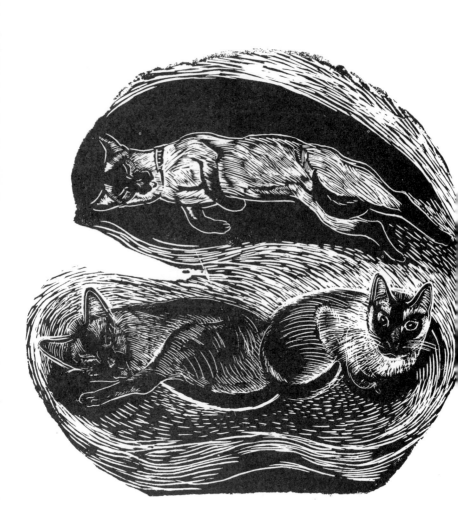

Enid Marx

Christopher Cunliffe

This started off as a joke portrait of our own dear cat, *Sam*, disapproving of us going off to *another* Craft Fair; but it seemed a bit rude to immortalise him sulking, so it turned into a Universally Cross Cat instead. There he sits, brain the size of Betelgeux. . . .

Anne Jope

This print illustrates the following passages from *Rushavenn Time* by Theresa Whistler

'Rebecca heard the stove thrum, drawing hard in the wind, and the shutter in the round black stove-pipe, pushed as far shut as it would go, clinked in the down-gusts. A little woodsmoke puffed out at each clink and stung her eyes, blueing the shadows . . . .

Over the high mantelshelf stood an old, dark-painted fan, out-spread between the tea-caddy and the brass candlestick. Beside it lay another, its pair, with ivory ends and a silk tassel – shut . . .

There were not many ornaments, though a little well-kept brass winked here and there. In one corner hung a long leather apron with the bow-saw and hedging-hook and bill-hook. At the end of the mantelshelf perched a wooden decoy-pigeon, carefully painted . . .

But the crowded feel of it was mainly because of piles and piles of newspapers and magazines stacked againt the walls, even filling up the vacant seats at the bench which ran round two sides of the table. The half-wild cats sat on thrones of yellowing journals. The satiny, dingy-white terrier under the ancient oak settle had his den between two more squat pillars of the same . . .'

Clifford Webb

50

Joan Hassall

Joan Hassall

William Rawlinson

Felix, and *Rufus* who lies across the endpapers of this book, were brothers and were orphaned at one month old. Rescued from drowning, they became very much loved. Rufus had six claws on each foot and could use them like human hands.

Sybella Stiles

Tigger, country tabby and arch-thief in his basket on the kitchen boiler, waiting for some delicate morsel to be left unattended.

Miriam Macgregor

The elderly *Archie Alcock* and *Comfrey Larkham*, 1988. This is not as unkind as it looks, since *someone*, woken by yowls at 5 am, kindly got up and let Comfrey out – and who was to know that it would snow? Archie died on New Year's Eve at a great age and Comfrey now tolerates a large dog.

Miriam Macgregor

A question of territory.

Paula Rudall

Reynolds Stone

Ann Tout

Maltese Cat. The sharp early morning sun shines on a deserted waterside; all that moves is the sea, a lone fisherman, and cats, laid-out cats and curled-up cats, all beautiful shapes to engrave.

Francis Kilvert's cat Toby was a tabby. Whether he was as splendid a creature as my *Rowntree*, who posed for me when I was engraving the illustrations for the Gregynog Press, is not revealed. Rowntree and his brother *Cadbury*, who were so tiny and clutched each other so tightly when they came to us, looked unerringly like the picture on a box of chocolates.

Sheep, which appeared in whatever I engraved after 1980, have been superseded by cats it seems, I have to have animals near me and I draw them in any spare time. There is no room for our beloved sheep here and the foxes have eaten all our chickens, again, so it's just cats (and Sam, of course).

We had just moved house, and I had caught flu, when the anonymous black cat on the Frontispiece joined me in the only warm room, and appropriated a Jacob fleece in the only available chair.

Sarah van Niekerk

INDEX